POLLINATOR PALS

LEON THE LADYBUG POLLINATES

by Rebecca Donnelly
illustrated by Dean Gray

GRASSHOPPER

Tools for Parents & Teachers

Grasshopper Books enhance imagination and introduce the earliest readers to fiction with fun storylines and illustrations. The easy-to-read text supports early reading experiences with repetitive sentence patterns and sight words.

Before Reading

- Discuss the cover illustration. What do they see?
- Look at the glossary together. Discuss the words.

Read the Book

- Read the book to the child, or have him or her read independently.
- "Walk" through the book and look at the illustrations. Who is the main character? What is happening in the story?

After Reading

- Prompt the child to think more. Ask: Leon the ladybug is a predator. He hunts aphids. Can you think of other insects that are predators? What do they hunt?

Grasshopper Books are published by Jump!
5357 Penn Avenue South
Minneapolis, MN 55419
www.jumplibrary.com

Library of Congress Cataloging-in-Publication Data

Names: Donnelly, Rebecca, author.
Gray, Dean, illustrator.
Title: Leon the ladybug pollinates / by Rebecca Donnelly; illustrated by Dean Gray.
Description: Minneapolis, MN: Jump!, Inc., [2022]
Series: Pollinator pals
Includes reading tips and supplementary back matter.
Audience: Ages 7-10.
Identifiers: LCCN 2021001289 (print)
LCCN 2021001290 (ebook)
ISBN 9781636902340 (hardcover)
ISBN 9781636902357 (paperback)
ISBN 9781636902364 (ebook)
Subjects: LCSH: Readers (Primary)
Ladybugs–Juvenile fiction.
Classification: LCC PE1119.2 .D675 2022 (print)
LCC PE1119.2 (ebook)
DDC 428.6/2–dc23
LC record available at https://lccn.loc.gov/2021001289
LC ebook record available at https://lccn.loc.gov/2021001290

Editor: Eliza Leahy
Direction and Layout: Anna Peterson
Illustrator: Dean Gray

Printed in the United States of America at Corporate Graphics in North Mankato, Minnesota.

Table of Contents

On the Hunt

Hi, I'm Leon. I'm a ladybug. People also call me a lady beetle even though I'm a male. Some ladybugs are plain, but I have spots. Can you count them?

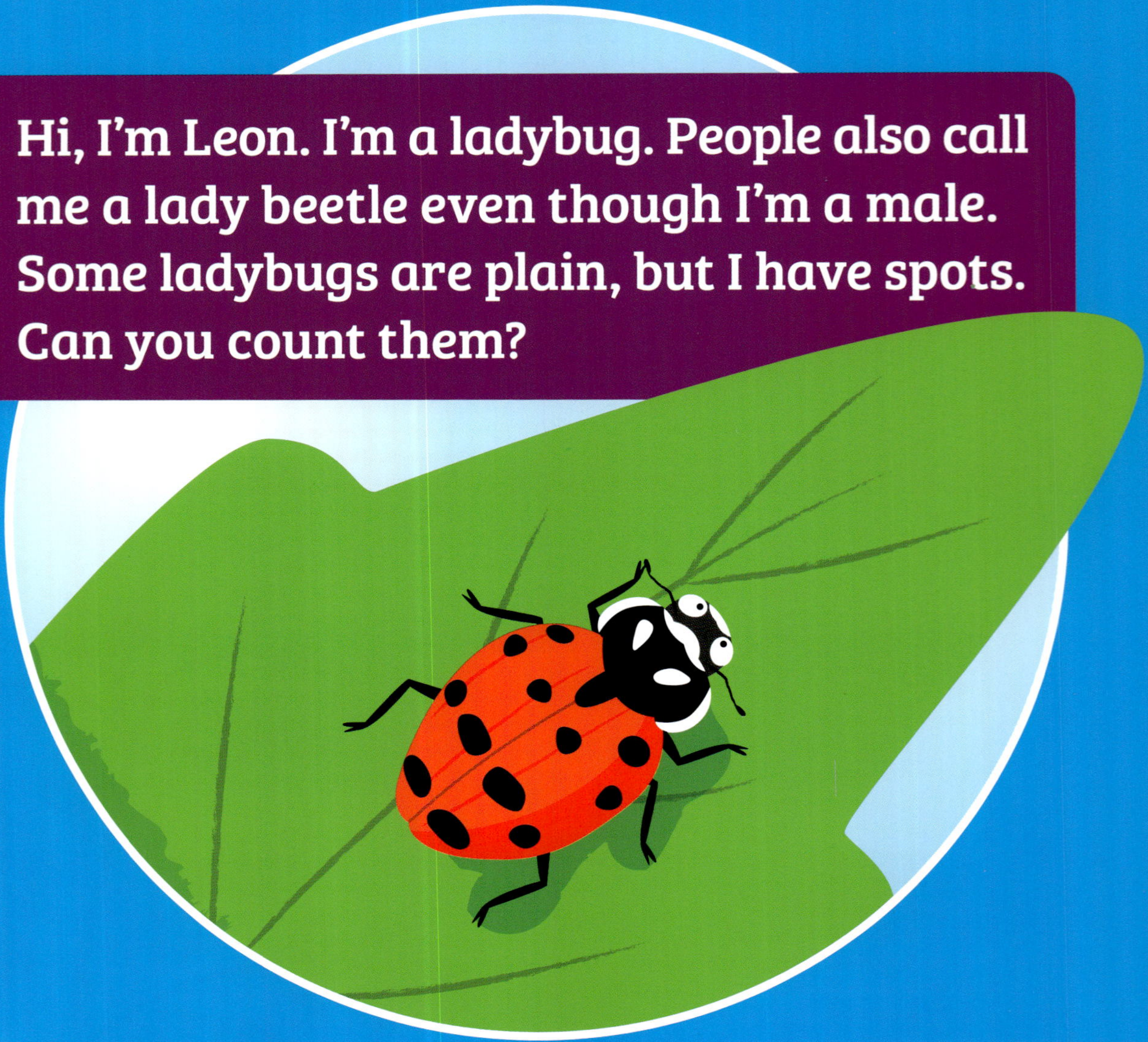

Insects like me are cold-blooded. I need the warm sun to wake me up in the morning. Let's get moving!

I might look cute, but my bright color warns bigger insects and birds to stay away. If that doesn't work, I make a bad smell with my legs. Yuck! No one wants to eat me.

I'm hungry. It's time to hunt. My favorite food is a tiny insect called an aphid. I can eat dozens of them each day.

Gardeners like me because
aphids eat their plants.
I help keep gardens healthy.

This tomato plant is a good place to find aphids. I walk all over its leaves and blossoms. Some pollen sticks to my legs and body. There's an aphid! *Munch!*

Sometimes I eat pollen and nectar, too.

This blossom has some tasty nectar inside. More pollen sticks to my legs!

pollen

I'm ready to fly to another plant. I open my hard outer wings. They are called elytra. I use the soft wings underneath to fly. Watch me go!

I hunt aphids on many plants in the garden. Do you like roses and sunflowers?

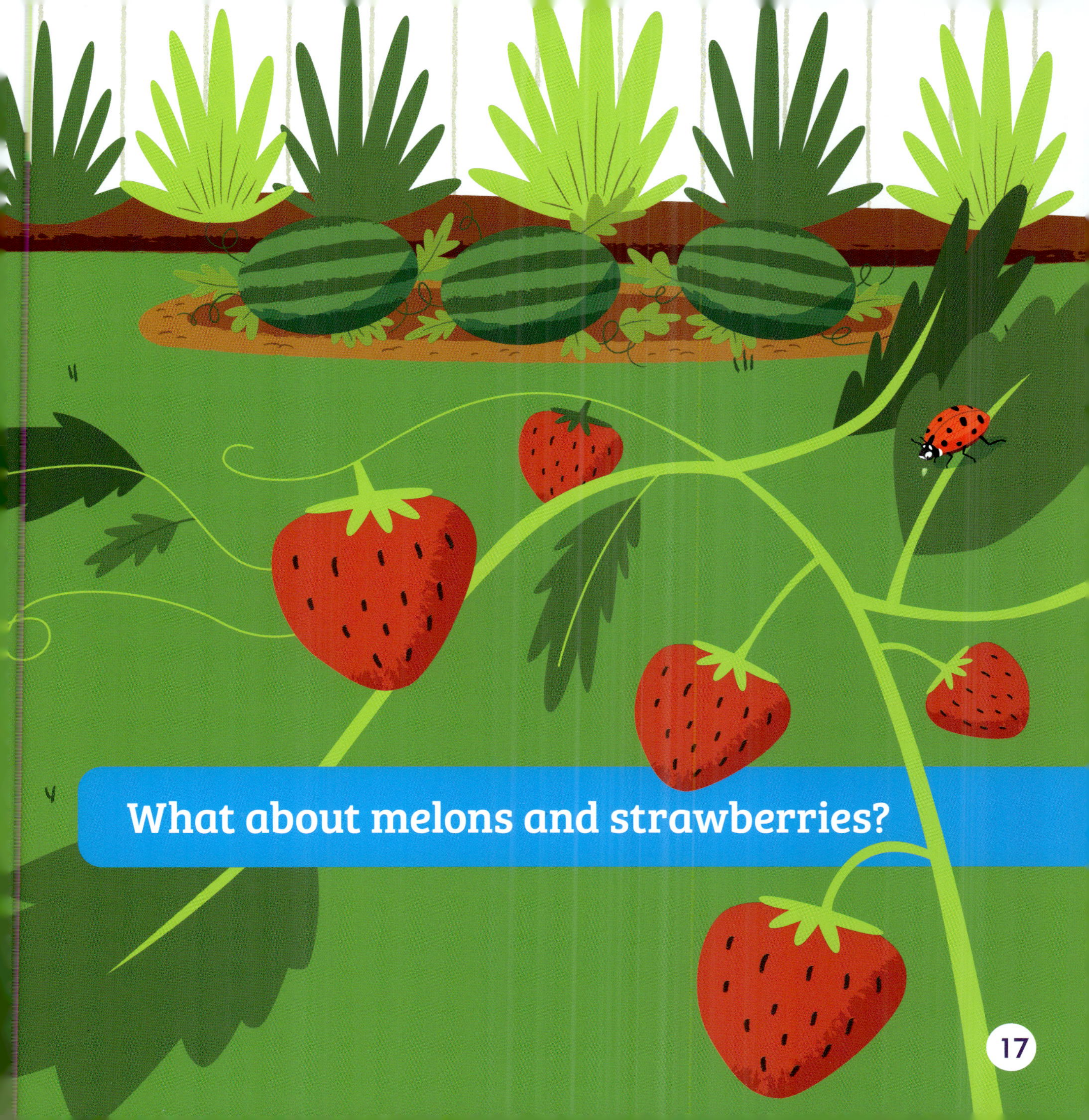

What about melons and strawberries?

When I land to hunt aphids, some of the pollen comes off and sticks to the blossoms. That's how I pollinate!

The pollen I leave behind helps seeds grow. New plants grow from the seeds.

In the fall, I migrate to the mountains. I stop along the way to eat a little extra nectar and spread more pollen.

Thousands of us hibernate together during the winter. We will be back in spring!

Let's Review!

Ladybugs spread pollen as they hunt aphids. Let's see how Leon does it!

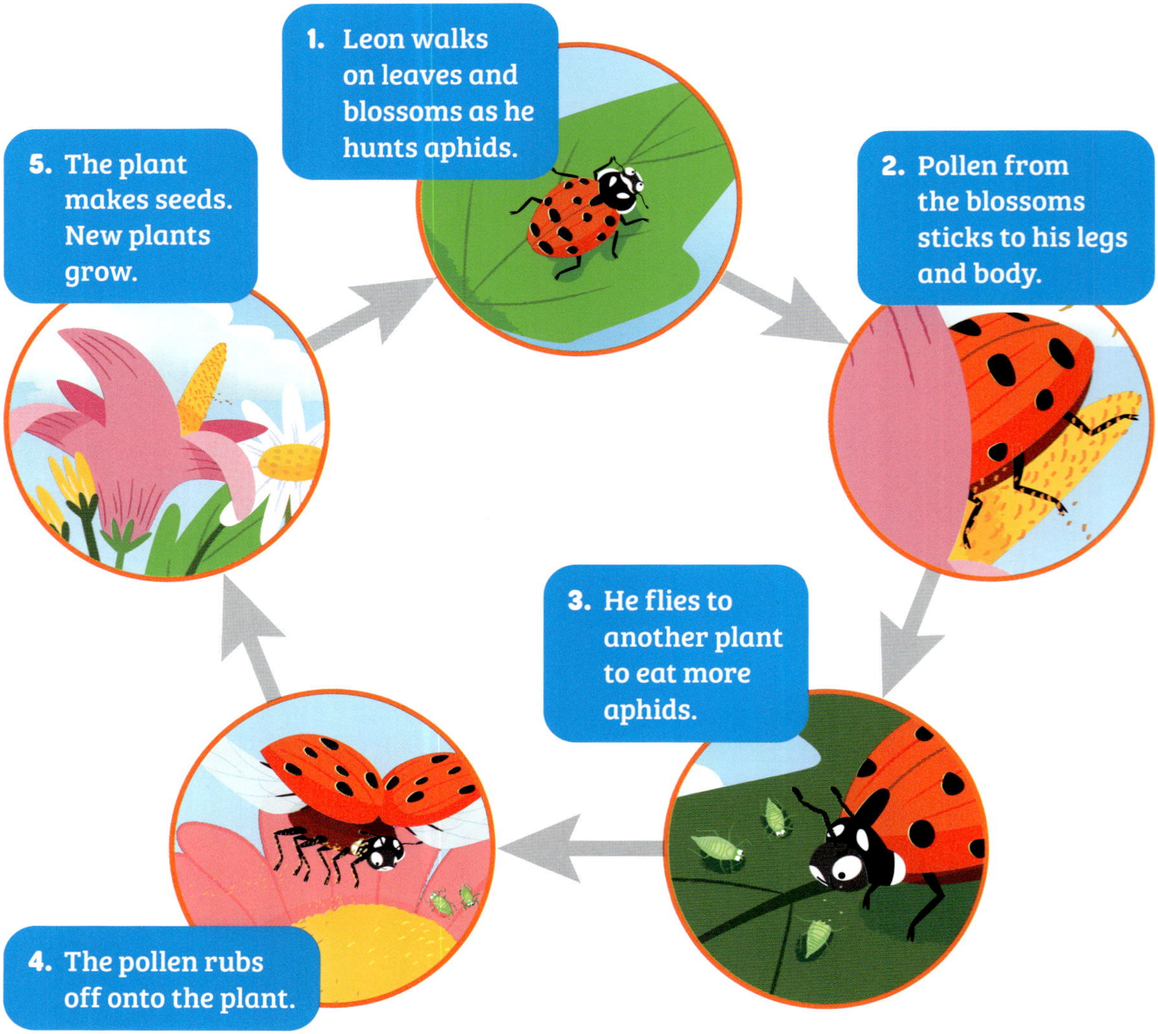

Where Convergent Ladybugs Live

Leon is a convergent ladybug. Take a look at where convergent ladybugs live!

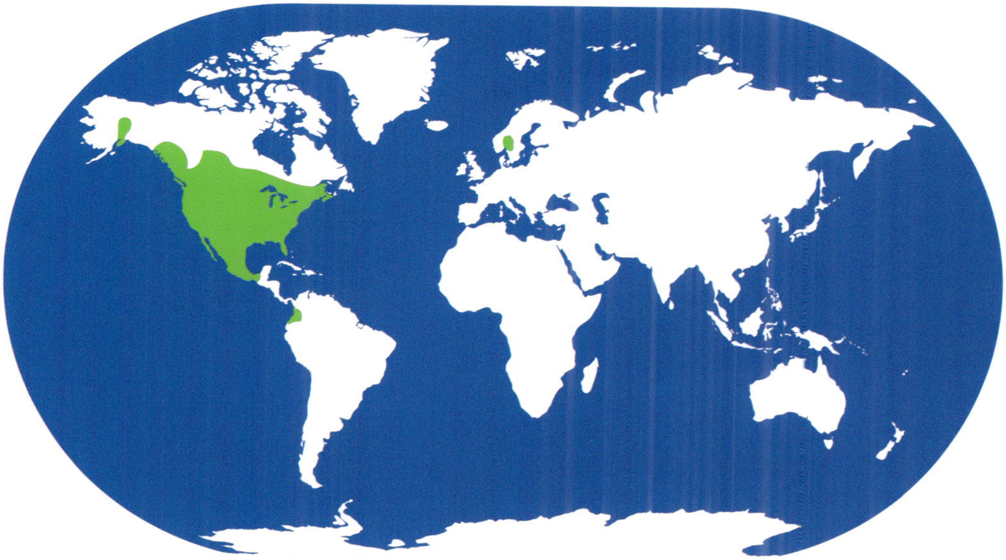

■ = where convergent ladybugs live

To Learn More

Finding more information is as easy as 1, 2, 3.

1. Go to www.factsurfer.com
2. Enter "**Leontheladybugpollinates**" into the search box.
3. Choose your book to see a list of websites.

Glossary

aphid: A small insect that damages plants and crops by sucking sap from their leaves.

blossoms: Flowers on trees and bushes.

cold-blooded: Needing heat from a source like the sun to stay warm.

elytra: The hard outer wings of a ladybug.

hibernate: To be inactive during all or part of the winter.

migrate: To move to another area or climate at a particular time of year.

nectar: A sweet liquid made by flowers to attract pollinators.

pollen: A powder made by the male parts of plants.

pollinate: To take pollen from the male part of a flower and put it on the female part of a flower so the plant can reproduce.

Index